QUILT
BOOK OF DAYS

Illustrations by
Penny Brown

Photography by
Claude Simon

A Sterling/Museum Quilts Book
Sterling Publishing Co., Inc. New York

Opposite and cover: SNOW CRYSTALS, Oklahoma c.1930

Published by Sterling Publishing Company, Inc.
387 Park Avenue South, New York, NY 10016
And by Museum Quilts Publications
254-258 Goswell Road, London EC1V 7EB
Distributed in Canada by Sterling Publishing
c/o Canadian Manda Group, P.O. Box 920, Station U
Toronto, Ontario, Canada M8Z 5P9
Distributed in Australia by Capricorn Link Ltd.
P.O. Box 665 Lane Cove, NSW 2066

All the quilts featured in this book are from the Susan Jenkins Collection

Copyright © 1993 by Museum Quilts Publications

All rights reserved. No part of this publication may be reproduced or transmitted
in any form or by any means, electronic or mechanical, including photocopy, recording,
or any information storage and retrieval system now known or to be invented
without permission in writing from the publishers

Design by Bet Ayer
Photographs styled by Sonia Cauvin

Printed and bound in Korea

ISBN: 1 897954 03 4

Princess Feather c.1870

· JANUARY ·

1

2

3

4

· JANUARY ·

5

6

7

8

9

· JANUARY ·

10

11

 · JANUARY ·

12

13

 · JANUARY ·

14

15

16

17

18

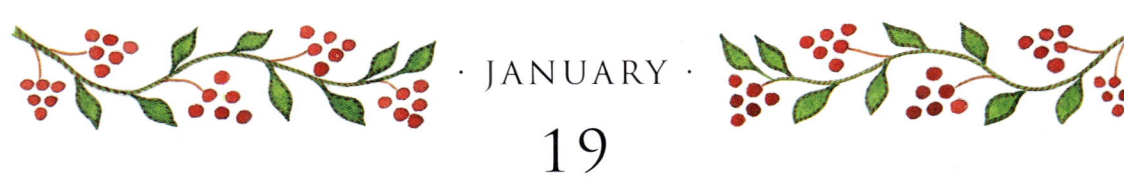

· JANUARY ·

19

20

21

22

23

 · JANUARY ·

24

25

 · JANUARY ·

26

27

JANUARY

28

29

30

31

Pennsylvania Dutch Folk Art Quilt c.1880

· FEBRUARY ·

1

2

3

4

· FEBRUARY ·

5

6

FEBRUARY

7

8

9

10

11

 · FEBRUARY ·

12

13

 · FEBRUARY ·

14

15

16

17

18

· FEBRUARY ·

19

20

21

22

23

 · FEBRUARY ·

24

25

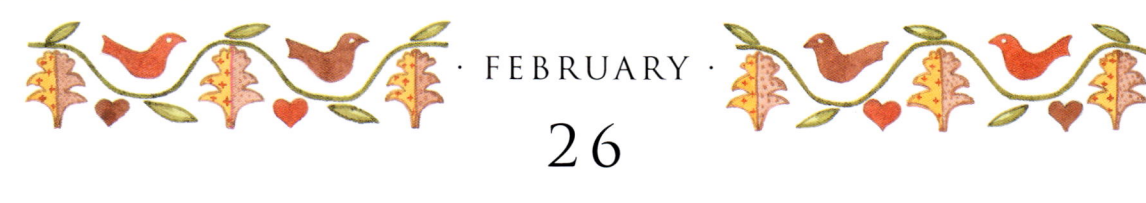

· FEBRUARY ·

26

27

28

29

· MARCH ·

1

2

3

4

Stars c.1900

 · MARCH ·

5

6

7

8

9

 · MARCH ·

10

11

 · MARCH ·

12

13

14

15

16

· MARCH ·

17

18

19

20

21

 · MARCH ·

22

23

 · MARCH ·

24

25

26

27

28

· MARCH ·

29

30

31

· APRIL ·

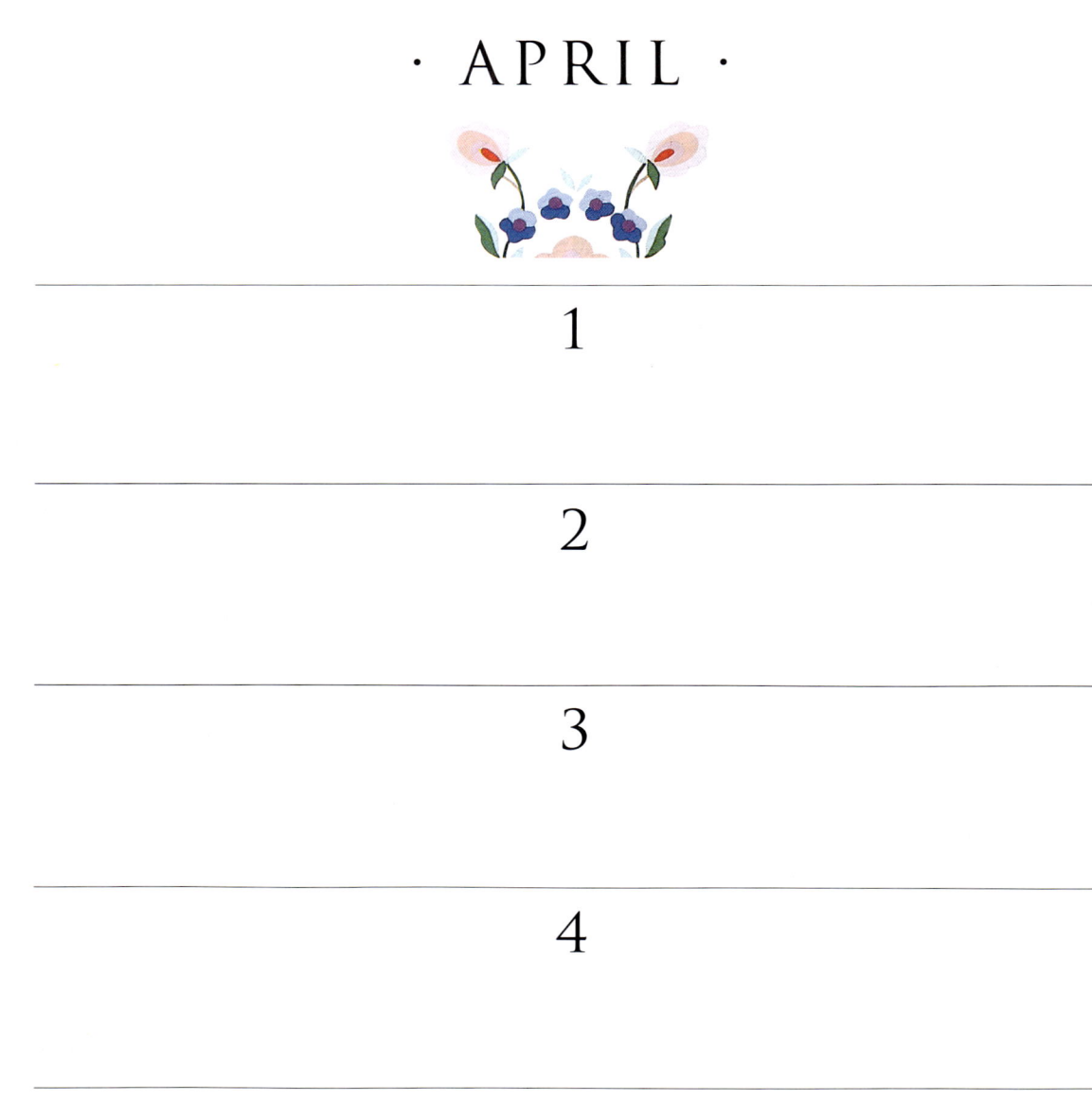

1

2

3

4

Paradise Tree Appliqué c.1930

 · APRIL ·

5

6

7

8

9

 · APRIL ·

10

11

 · APRIL ·

12

13

 · APRIL ·

14

15

16

17

18

· APRIL ·

19

20

21

22

23

 · APRIL ·

24

25

26

 · APRIL ·

27

28

29

30

· MAY ·

1

2

3

4

Iris c.1930

· MAY ·

5

6

7

8

9

 · MAY ·

10

11

 · MAY ·

12

13

14

15

16

· MAY ·

17

18

19

20

21

 · MAY ·

22

23

 · MAY ·

24

25

26

 · MAY ·

27

28

29

30

31

· JUNE ·

1

2

3

4

Love Apple c.1880

 · JUNE ·

5

6

7

8

9

 · JUNE ·

10

11

 · JUNE ·

12

13

14

15

16

 · JUNE ·

17

18

 · JUNE ·

19

20

 · JUNE ·

21

22

23

24

25

 · JUNE ·

26

27

28

29

30

· JULY ·

1

2

3

4

Shooting Stars c.1930

· JULY ·

5

6

7

8

9

 · JULY ·

10

11

12

13

14

 · JULY ·

15

16

 · JULY ·

17

18

 · JULY ·

19

20

21

22

23

 · JULY ·

24

25

26

27

28

 · JULY ·

29

30

31

· AUGUST ·

1

2

3

4

String of Flags c.1900

· AUGUST ·

5

6

7

8

9

 · AUGUST ·

10

11

 · AUGUST ·

12

13

14

 · AUGUST ·

15

16

17

18

19

 · AUGUST ·

20

21

22

23

24

 · AUGUST ·

25

26

27

· AUGUST ·

28

29

30

31

· SEPTEMBER ·

1

2

3

4

Baskets c.1870

SEPTEMBER

5

6

7

8

9

SEPTEMBER

10

11

 SEPTEMBER

12

13

14

15

16

SEPTEMBER

17

18

19

20

21

SEPTEMBER

22

23

SEPTEMBER

24

25

26

SEPTEMBER

27

28

29

30

· OCTOBER ·

1

2

3

4

Rose Wreath c.1880

 · OCTOBER ·

5

6

7

8

9

· OCTOBER ·

10

11

· OCTOBER ·

12

13

14

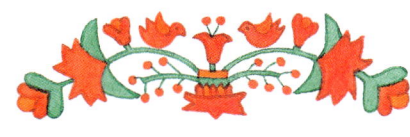 · OCTOBER ·

15

16

17

18

19

 · OCTOBER ·

20

21

22

23

24

· OCTOBER ·

25

26

27

 · OCTOBER ·

28

29

30

31

· NOVEMBER ·

1

2

3

4

Amish Evergreen c.1940

 NOVEMBER

5

6

7

8

9

NOVEMBER

10

11

NOVEMBER

12

13

14

15

16

 NOVEMBER

17

18

19

20

21

NOVEMBER

22

23

NOVEMBER

24

25

26

27

28

 NOVEMBER

29

30

· DECEMBER ·

1

2

3

4

Log Cabin c.1930

· DECEMBER ·

5

6

7

8

9

 · DECEMBER ·

10

11

· DECEMBER ·

12

13

14

15

16

· DECEMBER ·

17

18

19

 · DECEMBER ·

20

21

22

 · DECEMBER ·

23

24

25

26

27

· DECEMBER ·

28

29

30

31